Envision It! | Visual Skills Handbook

Author's Purpose

Cause and Effect

Compare and Contrast

Sequence

Author's Purpose

Inform

Entertain

Cause and Effect

Cause

Effect

Compare and Contrast

Sequence

Envision It! | Visual Strategies Handbook

Background Knowledge

Let's Think About Reading!

- What do I already know?
- What does this remind me of?

Important Ideas

Let's **Think** About **Reading!**

- What is important to know?

Inferring

Let's **Think** About **Reading!**

- What do I already know?
- How does this help me understand what happened?

Monitor and Clarify

Let's **Think** About **Reading!**

- What does not make sense?
- How can I fix it?

Predict and Set Purpose

Trains

Let's Think About Reading!

- What do I already know?
- What do I think will happen?
- What is my purpose for reading?

Questioning

Let's **Think** About **Reading!**

- What questions do I have about what I am reading?

Story Structure

Beginning

Middle

End

Let's Think About Reading!

- What happens in the beginning?
- What happens in the middle?
- What happens in the end?

Summarize

The dog knocked over the table.

Let's Think About Reading!

- What happens in the story?
- What is the story mainly about?

Text Structure

Let's Think About Reading!

- How is the story organized?
- Are there any patterns?

Visualize

 About **Reading!**

- What pictures do I see in my mind?